PEGAN DIET COOKBOOK

Delicious Recipes: Pegan, Vegan, Paleo, Gluten-free, Dairy-free, and More --- The Path to Lifelong Health!

STEPH MILLER

Table of Contents

Introduction

Most people have no idea of what a Pegan diet is; they are not to be blamed since a Pegan diet is something completely non-mainstream. A Pegan diet is a relatively new type of diet that was first introduced in 2015 by Dr. Mark Hyman, the Director of the Cleveland Clinic Center for Functional Medicine. This type of diet offers the best of both vegan and paleo diets.

Of course, this combination may be a tad difficult to understand.How can a diet that consists of protein-rich foods like meat and seafood pair up with a vegan diet that prohibits the consumption of animal-based foods like eggs, meats, and dairy products? Apparently, Mark Hyman has managed to find a middle ground and has formulated the pegan diet.

A Pegan diet encourages you to remove foods that contain high starch and sugar content from your diet and replace them with foods that provide good fat. Additionally, there is no abstinence from animal-based foods. Therefore, you can say that a Pegan diet would consist of healthy oils, seeds, nuts, vegetables, and fruits, along with sustainable meat, low-mercury content fishes, poultry, and eggs. However, the question here is how much of these food groups you need to consume?

The diet should be based on the 75-25 rule. This means that 75% of your diet should constitute of vegetables, fruits, and other plant-based foods. The rest 25% will include animal-based foods. When you are segregating the proteins, you need to ensure that you also include protein sources for the first 75% of the diet like seeds, nuts, and legumes. As for meat, it is advised that you cut down a portion of the meat little by little daily.

According to Dr. Mark Hyman, the most pressing concern about our food system can be driven by chronic diseases. He also believes that the minority and poor populations often bear the brunt of corporate food manufacturers. Overall, Hyman cites that bad food practices are the root causes of such issues.

So, how is the Pegan diet different than other diets? Yes, most diets include plant-based and animal-based foods in varying proportions. These proportions are designed based on your body requirements.

If you think that shifting to a Pegan diet will be a tough transition, it is nothing to worry about. Luckily, a Pegan diet has a lot of similarities with other types of diets. For instance, if you compare a Pegan diet with a vegan diet, the similarities here are that both diets include plant-based foods and shun dairy products. In the case of a paleo diet, even the Pegan diet includes the consumption of animal-based foods.However, the difference here is that you should only consume these foods in small portions.

As you can see, a Pegan diet mixes the best of most diet types and offers a very healthy alternative. You get the best of the best so that your body remains healthy. A Pegan diet is all about whole foods that are natural or very minimally processed. With the help of this diet, you will have a healthy diet without having to sacrifice the flexibility on both types of diets. A Pegan diet scores good grades for people who prefer consuming real foods and avoiding packaged foods.

In this book, we will also be talking about some ground rules of this diet. Now, any type of diet you follow will have its set of rules. For instance, you cannot consume animal- and dairy-based products if you are following a vegan diet. You may have heard the saying 'you are what you eat' – this statement is quite true. It is very important to follow dietary guidelines because the food and beverages we consume help fuel our body and provide nutrients.

In this book, we have also mentioned 16 golden rules of following a Pegan diet. Most of these guidelines are penned down by Dr. Mark Hyman to promote a healthy diet for children and adults and prevent chronic diseases.

These rules have been designed to improve health and lower the chances of developing various chronic diseases ranging from diabetes to cardiovascular diseases. These rules are a general blueprint for good nutrition and healthy eating.

This guide also includes the Pegan diet products that need to be in your shopping cart. These include a wide variety of fruits and vegetables, meat, seafood, oils, etc. The products have been chosen specifically because of their nutritional value. There is also a one-week Pegan meal plan to get you started with this diet. You can follow it till you make your own Pegan meal plan as per your food preferences.

Lastly, we will share some lip-smacking recipes with you. In this section, you will provide you with the ingredients and cooking methods used to prepare your breakfast, entrees, sides, desserts, soups, and salads. All the ingredients used to cook these delicious meals will not harm your health in any way.

CHAPTER 1: HOW THE PEGAN DIET IS DIFFERENT FROM OTHER POPULAR DIETS?

A Pegan diet can be considered as a cross-breed between different types of diets. However, it is still different from them all. Let us learn how a Pegan diet differs from other types of popular diets:

- **Paleo**

By definition, a paleo diet is a concept that believes that the body works best when we eat the way our ancestors did. This diet included limited amounts of nuts and seeds, healthy oils, fruits, vegetables, and meat. It did not allow anything artificial, dairy products, beans, potatoes, grains (including corn), and processed foods. Meats that are consumed are often lean and there would not any agricultural growing of crops and grains. In most cases, grass-fed and organic foods would be the majority of the diet.

On the other hand, a Pegan diet takes the best of paleo and vegan diets and combines them. In short, you consume healthy oils, fruits, vegetables, and meats in smaller helpings and avoid added sugars, gluten, and dairy.

One of the biggest misconceptions of a paleo diet is that the diet mainly consists of 'meat'. Logically, it would have been impossible for cavemen to have a diet that comprised only of meat. Taking down large animals is not easy and a lot of time would be spent on hunting these animals down. Therefore, our ancestors also started eating other nutrient-dense foods like nuts, legumes, fruits, and vegetables as a supplement.

However, this is where the similarities between a Pegan and a paleo diet ends. In the case of a paleo diet, losing weight is much more difficult because you are still eating gluten-free grains like rice, corn, and oats, which adds a lot of extra calories. In the case of a Pegan diet, you are not consuming more than a single serving of gluten.

- **Vegan**

A vegan diet and a Pegan diet are almost similar – the only difference is that a vegan diet is 100% plant-based while a Pegan diet needs to be at least 75% of what you put on your plate. A vegan diet is defined as a way of living that excludes all forms of animal-based products for various purposes like clothing, foods, etc. Hence, a vegan diet is devoid of animal food products like dairy, eggs, and meats.

People choose to follow a vegan diet for various reasons ranging from environmental to ethical concerns. However, they can also stem from the desire to improve health.

On the other hand, a Pegan diet is almost a vegan diet. Instead of eating fruits and vegetables as side dishes, a Pegan diet has animal-based products as the side dishes. The main aspects of this diet consist of everything vegetarian. Additionally, a Pegan diet also discourages dairy products.

From the above, we understand that a vegan diet is very much similar to a Pegan diet. However, you exclude meat, poultry, and fish from your diet in the case of a vegan diet. Additionally, vegans also exclude other types of animal-based products from their lifestyles and diets like honey and eggs; this also includes any other products that contain animal by-products like leather, wool, cosmetics, etc. In the case of a Pegan diet, animal-based products are allowed for consumption; however, these dishes need to compose of only 25% of your plate; the rest 75% needs to be plant-based foods.

- **Vegetarian**

Some people may opt for a plant-based diet and not choose to consume meat for a variety of reasons. By definition, a vegan diet is a diet that excludes all food sources that are derived from animal sources like eggs, dairy, seafood, fish, poultry, and meat. Similarly, a vegetarian diet excludes all animal-based products like seafood, fish, poultry, and meat. However, they are allowed to consume some forms of animal-based products like dairy.

When you compare a vegetarian diet with the Pegan diet, there are a lot of similarities. For instance, both types of diets include plant-based foods. However, this is where the similarities end. When you are on a Pegan diet, you are not allowed to consume any dairy products like butter, milk, etc. Additionally, you are also not allowed to consume grains, whether they are whole or refined.

Unlike the Pegan diet, you are also not allowed to consume other types of animal-based products like meat, eggs, and meat. However, this also depends on the type of vegetarian diet you are following. For instance, a flexitarian diet, or also known as a semi-vegetarian diet, allows you to consume dairy products and eggs; it also includes small amounts of seafood, fish, poultry, and meat. Then, there is the Pescatarian diet where you cannot consume poultry and meat; however, you can eat seafood, fish, dairy products, and eggs.

- **Keto**

A Pegan diet and a keto diet are both about plant-based diets; however, the emphasis is different. A ketogenic diet is a strong bias towards plant-based foods; on the other hand, a Pegan diet has a similar bias towards the paleo plan. While there are many similarities between the two, there are also some key differences.

A keto diet was developed by the famous functional medical practitioner, Will Cole. He eventually converted to keto diets after seeing their effectiveness on his patients. While some people practice a keto diet with a lot of animal fats and products, Cole adjusted the diet in a way that it only included fish as the only source of animal protein.

Yes, it is possible to do a vegan-only version of the keto diet because the diet is defined as whether you are in nutritional ketosis. Based on theory, it does not matter how you reach the ketosis state; you can get into ketosis with junk food as well as healthy food.

Both types of diets aim at controlling blood sugar levels and reducing inflammation. For most parts, both diets eschew legumes, grains, meat, and dairy. The best aspect of these diets is that the boundaries are squishy – neither programs are extreme or doctrinaire. Additionally, both types of diets allow you to consume 'forbidden' foods occasionally if it does not cause any problem. In most cases, you cannot go wrong with both types of diets.

- **DASH**

The DASH diet, or the Dietary Approaches to Stop Hypertension, is a diet that has been designed to treat high blood pressure without the requirement of any medication. This type of diet is also followed for preventing other types of health problems like diabetes, stroke, heart disease, cancer, and osteoporosis.

A typical DASH diet consists of nuts, poultry, fish, whole grains, low-fat dairy, fruits, and vegetables, which is almost similar to a Mediterranean diet. However, this diet limits the intake of sodium – not more than 2,300mg of salt per day. While this diet does not lead to weight loss, many people also notice this decrease in weight because they are promoting healthier choices.

When compared to the Pegan diet, both diets have a lot of similarities. Fruits, vegetables, and animal-based products make a part of your meal. However, you need to ensure that the meat is lean in the case of the DASH diet; on the other hand, eggs, poultry, and meat needs to be sustainably raised, organic, and grass-fed in the case of a Pegan diet. While nuts are consumed in both diets, whole grains are not included in a Pegan diet, as compared to a DASH diet.

Additionally, a Pegan diet also discourages dairy products while a DASH diet does allow consumption of a low-fat diet. The differences between both types of diet narrow down to the result – people that practice DASH diets often suffer from health problems like high blood pressure and the foods mentioned prevent such conditions.

- **Mediterranean Diet**

When you look at it closely, there are not a lot of differences between a Mediterranean diet and a Pegan diet. It has been documented that a Mediterranean diet offers a lot of benefits ranging from decreased inflammation and weight loss to lower risk of chronic diseases and illnesses.

Based on studies, it has been found that a Mediterranean diet, coupled with no smoking and daily exercises, will prevent 90% of Type-2 diabetes, 90% of coronary heart diseases, and 7% of stroke. All you need to do is follow the healthy food choices that are consistent with a traditional Mediterranean diet.

When it comes to comparing the Mediterranean diet with a Pegan diet, you will notice that both types of diets revolve around healthier eating plans. Both diets emphasize eating more vegetables and fruits. A Mediterranean diet follows the principle of the paleo diet of staying away from packaged or processed foods.

The only difference between the two diets is the quality of animal products; the meat needs to be pasture-raised, wild, and organic. Additionally, a Pegan diet also eliminates refined foods like bread and whole wheat. Dairy products are also avoided in a Pegan diet.

Chapter 2: Top 16 Pegan Diet Rules

As mentioned above, the Pegan diet is inspired by two popular types of diets – the paleo and vegan diet. According to Dr. Hyman, this diet aims at promoting optimal health by balancing the blood sugar level and reducing inflammation. If you want to understand the rules of following a Pegan diet, they include:

1. Choose Seasonal Vegetables and Fruits

The primary food group for a Pegan diet is fruits and vegetables – they need to comprise 75% of your plate. In fact, they need to be an important part of your daily diet. They contain minerals and vitamins that will keep you healthy and protect you against diseases.

Most people would benefit from eating more vegetables and fruits for a more active, healthy, regular, and balanced lifestyle. Vegetables and fruits contain various types of minerals and vitamins that are good for your health like folic acid, phosphorus, zinc, magnesium, and various types of vitamins like E, C, A (beta-carotene), etc.

Fruits and vegetables are also low in sugar, salt, and fat. They are important sources of dietary fibers and are low in calories. With the help of fruits and vegetables, you will be able to maintain a healthy weight and reduce obesity. Additionally, you will also lower your blood pressure and cholesterol.

Fruits and vegetables contain powerful phytochemicals that help protect your overall health. Phytochemicals are mostly related to color – this means that vegetables and fruits that have different colors like white, blue-purple, red, yellow-orange, and green contain their own combination of nutrients and phytochemicals that work together to promote good health. For instance, white vegetables like cauliflower contain sulforaphane and may help protect against certain types of cancers; on the other hand, green vegetables like kale and spinach contain zeaxanthin and lutein that protect against age-related health problems like eye diseases. We will talk more about the Rainbow diet later in this section.

If you want to maximize nutrient intake, it is important to consume different types of fruits and vegetables. You can try buying fruits and vegetables based on the seasons; this is nature's way to ensure that your body gets a healthy mix of plant chemicals and nutrients. Alternatively, you can also choose to buy different fruits and vegetables and try out new recipes.

2. Quality is Important

Foods that are included in a Pegan diet are known as real foods – these foods are rich in nutrients, free of chemical additives, and mostly unprocessed. In essence, these are the types of foods that the first human civilizations used to eat. Sadly, processed foods became popular in the 20th century and shifted drastically towards ready-to-eat foods.

While processed foods are convenient and quick, they are also harmful to the human body. In fact, eating real foods of high quality can be one of the most important things you can do for your body to maintain a high-quality life and good health. The quality of the foods you eat will dictate your overall health.

In the case of any diet, the quality of the foods and ingredients are very important. Similarly, the quality of the foods for a Pegan diet needs to be nothing but the best. A typical Pegan plate needs to have 2-3 fresh cups of produce – it needs to include leafy, dark greens, and other non-starchy vegetables. If you want to get the maximum nutritional density, it is recommended that you also add herbs and a variety of colorful vegetables and fruits. In the case of a Pegan diet, emphasis on the quality is an important nutritional factor – therefore, it is recommended that you always opt for organic and locally-grown foods whenever possible.

A Pegan diet also consists of some animal-based products. However, these dishes are meant to be used as side dishes to the plant-based main courses. The eggs, poultry, and red meat need to be sustainably raised or grass-fed. The fish should be caught in the wild and have lower mercury levels.

Omega-3 fatty acids also make up some part of a Pegan diet; omega-3 fat sources are known to be highly anti-inflammatory. These foods mostly include seafood, which needs to be wild-caught fatty fishes like herring, mackerel, anchovies, sardines, and salmon.

3. Plant Foods Should Equal 75% of Your Total Food Consumption

A Pegan diet is a combination of a paleo diet and a vegan diet. The paleo diet consists of whole foods that our ancestors hunted and gathered, like vegetables, fruits, nuts, and occasionally meat. On the other hand, the vegan diet means you only eat plant-based foods.

By principle, a Pegan diet is a diet that consists of 75% foods that are plant-based, with animal-based proteins comprising of the remaining 25%. These food sources need to be whole and sustainably produced while limiting their effect on the environment.

While there have been no in-depth studies that prove the benefits of a Pegan diet, experts are gaining more data that proves that the semi-plant-based diet is good for your health. Since a plant-based diet focuses on vegetables and fruits that are low in starch and high in fiber, a Pegan diet is said to be the most perfect type of diet today. It has also been studied that a plant-based diet will also lower bad cholesterol in the body and promote weight loss.

Vegetables and fruits are some of the most nutritionally diverse types of foods today – they have the most mineral and vitamin content that can help prevent diseases and reduce both inflammation and oxidative stress.

However, there are certain types of plant-based foods that you need to stay away from. For instance, white bread and rice are plant-based foods as well. However, they are highly processed; this means that they are void of body-healthy nutrients and have a high glycemic index. In turn, this can lead to increased hunger (which leads to overeating) and increased blood sugar levels.

The rest 25% of the diet consists of animal-based proteins. However, the servings need to be small; consider all the meat dishes to be side dishes. The meat sources need to be pasture-raised and grass-fed. As for seafood, it should be wild-caught and contain minimum mercury levels.

4. Eat the Rainbow

For the best nutritional intake, experts suggest that you should 'eat the rainbow'. As mentioned earlier, this implies that you eat colorful vegetables and fruits. These have a lot of benefits for the body.

Plants contain different types of pigments, or also known as phytonutrients. These phytonutrients give them a wide range of colors. Different-color vegetables and fruits have often been linked to specific health benefits and nutrients. While eating lots of fruits and vegetables is commendable, it is also important to focus on eating different-colored plants to increase the intake of various nutrients to benefit all areas of your overall health.

While there are many benefits of phytonutrients, it is not easy to perform randomized controlled trials – hence, researchers have based their research on the intakes and disease risk based on the population. As per these studies, it has been found that there are many benefits of eating colorful vegetables and fruits, with almost no downsides. By adding color to your Pegan diet, you will provide your body with an array of phytochemicals, minerals, and vitamins.

Let us look into some colors and check out their health benefits:

Red

Fruits and vegetables include grapefruit, pink guava, watermelon, tomato, etc.

Main phytonutrient: Lycopene (Vitamin A family)

Other minerals and vitamins:

- Vitamin K1
- Vitamin C
- Potassium
- Folate

Health benefits:

- Lowers risk of certain cancers
- Reduce sun-related skin damage
- Improves heart health

Yellow and orange

Fruits and vegetables include winter squash, pumpkin, bananas, tangerines, pineapple, carrots, yellow peppers, etc.

Main phytonutrient: Carotenoids (Vitamin A family)

Other minerals and vitamins:

- Vitamin C
- Potassium
- Vitamin A

- Folate
- Fiber

Health benefits:

- Lowers the risks of cancer
- Supports
- Eye health
- Improves heart health

Green

Fruits and vegetables include green herbs, Brussel sprouts, green cabbage, asparagus, avocados, broccoli, kale, spinach, etc.

Main phytonutrient: Carotenoids and chlorophyll in leafy greens and glucosinolates, isothiocyanates, and indoles in cruciferous greens (cabbage, broccoli)

Other minerals and vitamins:

- Vitamin K1
- Vitamin A
- Potassium
- Magnesium
- Folate
- Fiber

Health benefits:

- Lowers the risk of heart diseases and cancer
- Antioxidant
- Anti-inflammatory

5. Avoid Gluten

The terms 'gluten-free' and 'dairy-free' have been popping up everywhere in the past few years. Many people who are no longer dependent on gluten products have managed to control chronic diseases, food insensitivities, and inflammation. Dairy and gluten are common allergens that can cause a lot of health problems in people.

Gluten is a type of protein called prolamin and often found in grains like rye, barley, and wheat. Gluten is often referred to as a 'glue' that holds together baked products because it is known to be stretchy. There are many ways gluten can lead to inflammation in the body. This is because it contains high levels of anti-nutrients, which are proteins found in some types of plants. These anti-nutrients are not good for the body because they interfere with the natural absorption and digestion of food in the gut, thereby causing inflammation.

Consumption of gluten also leads to zonulin being released in the body. Zonulin is a type of protein in the body that controls the opening and closing of the junctions in the gut lining. Our gut is selectively permeable – it allows the good things to pass into the bloodstream while the bad things are kept away in the gut for removal. When you consume zonulin, it will interfere with the permeability of the gut and the junctions will remain open.

Dairy refers to animal milk like sheep's milk, goat's milk, cow's milk, and even camel's milk. Dairy is also found in a wide range of other products like butter, cheese, kefir, yogurt, and cream. Dairy is categorized as a type of allergenic food that is difficult to digest, which goes on to cause inflammation.

For instance, lactose intolerance is a condition that stems from dairy. Lactose is a sugar found in milk; to digest lactose, the body requires the production of the enzyme lactase. This enzyme is produced in the body in early childhood and we lose this ability as we age. This is a very common condition – over 65% of adults around the world are lactose intolerant.

Dairy products also contain casein, a protein that can cause problems in the immune system function and digestion, particularly A1 casein. If you think that lactose and A1 casein are causing digestive problems, you can look for other dairy alternatives. For instance, goat's milk contains less lactose than cow's milk.

6. Say No to Vegetable Oils

Not a lot of people know about this, but vegetable oils are bad for your health and the environment. Vegetable oils are oils that are extracted from various types of seeds like peanut, safflower, sunflower, corn, soybean, and rapeseed (canola oil). Unlike olive oil and coconut oil that is extracted by pressing, these vegetable oils are extracted in unnatural ways.

Apart from the continued myth about cholesterol and saturated fats, these oils are often advertised as healthy because they contain omega-3 fatty acids and monounsaturated fats. Promotions will often focus on these fake health claims. However, this does not paint the whole picture.

The reality here is that vegetable oils contain high concentrations of polyunsaturated fats (PUFAs); the human body contains 97% monounsaturated and saturated fats. The fat is required for hormone production and rebuilding cells. On the other hand, PUFAs are very unstable and oxidizes very quickly. In turn, this can cause mutation in cells and inflammation. The oxidation has also been linked to other types of diseases related to the heart.

Of course, we all know that omega-3 fatty acids are very healthy. However, it is the ratio between the omega-3 acids and the omega-6 acids that are important for good health.

Vegetable oils contain a lot of omega-6 fatty acids. These acids get oxidized very quickly. On the other hand, omega-3 fatty acids have been shown to protect against cancer and reduces inflammation.

Unbalanced levels of both types of acids have been linked to different types of cancers and other health problems.

Apart from the unnatural levels of omega-6 fatty acids and polyunsaturated fats, these vegetable oils contain many other things like chemicals, pesticides, and additives for processing. Some also contain BHT and BHA; these are natural antioxidants that prevent the food from spoiling quickly. However, studies have proven that they also produce potential cancer compounds in the body. Lastly, vegetable oil is also linked to other problems like kidney and liver damage, behavioral problems, infertility, and immune system issues.

7. Avoid Sugar and Eat Fruits in Moderation

Right from peanut butter to marinara sauce, added sugar is found on almost all products. Most people rely on processed foods from snacks and meals. However, these products also contain added sugar, which makes up a large proportion of their calorie intake.

According to dietary guidelines, it is suggested that you limit calorie intake from added sugar to a minimum of 10% daily. It has been concluded that excess sugar consumption is a lead cause of obesity and can also result in many chronic diseases like Type-2 diabetes.

The rates of obesity are increasing now more than ever; one of the main culprits is sugar-sweetened beverages. Sugar-sweetened drinks like sweet tea, juice, and soda contain fructose, a simple form of sugar. When you consume fructose, your hunger increases. Additionally, fructose also makes you more resistant to leptin, a hormone that regulates hunger and signals your body to stop eating.

In short, sugary beverages will not curb your hunger and you end up consuming high amounts of calories from liquids, which causes weight gain. It has been studied that people that drink sugary beverages weigh more than people who don't.

A high amount of sugar in your diet can also increase the risk of developing heart diseases. It has been studied that high-sugar diets can lead to inflammation, obesity, and increased blood pressure – all these are risk factors for various heart problems.

Increased sugar consumption has also been linked to acne. Foods that have a high glycemic index, like processed sugary treats, increases your blood sugar levels faster than foods that have low GMI. These foods will cause spikes in your insulin and blood sugar levels, which causes increased inflammation, oil production, and androgen secretion, all of which lead to acne. Additionally, population studies have shown that rural communities in the world that consume non-processed foods have almost no rates of acne, as compared to high-income and urban areas.

8. Avoid Gluten Grains

As mentioned above, gluten is a naturally occurring protein that is found in some grains like rye, barley, and wheat. This substance has a stretchy quality and holds the food together. Some other grams that contain gluten includes triticale, einkorn, Khorasan wheat, graham, farro, farina, semolina, emmer, durum, spelt, and wheat berries. While oats are naturally gluten-free, the gluten comes from cross-contamination when being processed with the grains listed previously. Other less obvious choices of gluten include modified food starch and soy sauce.

The thing that is not great about gluten is that it can cause side effects in some people. People react to gluten differently – when the body recognizes it as a toxin, it will deploy the immune cells to attack it. If you are sensitive to gluten and consume it accidentally, it will result in inflammation. The side effects can range from mild effects like diarrhea, alternating constipation, bloating, and fatigue to severe like intestinal damage, malnutrition, and unintentional weight loss.

It has been estimated that approximately one in every 113 Americans suffers from celiac disease; it has been concluded that people that suffer from celiac disease have a higher risk of anemia and osteoporosis. This also leads to other health problems like nerve disorders, infertility, and even cancer.

The good news here is that the damage can be reversed simply by eliminating gluten from your diet. Opting for a gluten-free diet is often the answer to celiac diseases. However, following a gluten-free diet is not easy; you may even need to take advice from a registered dietician to learn which foods contain gluten and also get other required nutrients from gluten-free alternatives.

In short, a gluten-free diet is a diet where you eliminate the consumption of foods that contain gluten. However, most whole grains that contain gluten also have nutrients like iron, magnesium, and vitamins. Therefore, it is important that you make up for these missing nutrients. For example, you can look into naturally gluten-free food products like poultry, eggs, fish, nuts, and whole fruits and vegetables.

9. Include Healthy Fats

Most people are unable to understand why monounsaturated and polyunsaturated fats are good for the body and why trans fats are bad. In fact, we have been aiming to remove fats from your diets whenever possible by switching to meals that contain low-fat levels. However, this change does not improve our health because we cut down on healthy fats with the bad fats.

While some fats are bad for the human body, some are important as well. Fats are one of the most important sources of energy for the human body. It will help absorb some minerals and vitamins. Fats also contribute towards the building of sheaths around the nerves and cell membranes. Fats are also useful for inflammation, muscle movement, and blood clotting. Therefore, some fats are better for the body in the long run.

Whether good or bad, all fats have a similar chemical structure. It consists of a chain where carbon atoms are bonded to hydrogen atoms. The difference between these fats lies only in the number and length and shape of the hydrogen and carbon atoms respectively.

Before getting into the good and healthy fats, let us get into the bad fats. Trans fat is considered the worst type of fat. This fat is created when healthy oils are turned into solids by a process of hydrogenation to prevent it from going rancid. This type of fat has no benefits for the health and not safe for consumption as well. In fact, trans fat has officially been banned in different countries like the US.

On the other hand, polyunsaturated and monounsaturated fats are good fats that come mainly from sources like fish, seeds, nuts, and vegetables. This type of fat remains in a liquid state at room temperature.

When you are dipping your bread in olive oil, you are getting monounsaturated fat. This fat has a single carbon-to-carbon double bond, which means that there are two fewer hydrogen atoms. This is why monounsaturated fats remain liquid at room temperature. Some great monounsaturated fat sources include sunflower oils, nuts, avocados, peanut oil, and olive oil.

10. Consume Clean Poultry, Meat, and Whole Eggs

As mentioned previously, meat and poultry are great sources of protein, especially for a Pegan diet. They also contain a lot of nutrients that your body requires like essential fatty acids, vitamins, zinc, iron, and iodine. Therefore, it is always a good idea to consume poultry, meat, and eggs as part of a Pegan diet. However, it is recommended that you stick with lean and unprocessed cuts to avoid consuming saturated fat and salt.

Eating clean is an amorphous term – it means that it carries no caloric or nutritional restrictions. While it is not easy to define what clean eating of whole eggs, meat, and poultry look like, the common thread appears to be – avoiding packaged and processed foods rich in artificial ingredients, salt, and sugar. This way, you end up choosing whole or real animal-based foods over refined ones.

Whole eggs, chicken and meat should be bought fresh, free of any artificial ingredients and unseasoned. By nature, these products are nutritionally dense, high in protein, and low in fat.

Once you have ensured that you have bought clean meat, cooking the products will kill all bacteria and other microorganisms. Apart from being healthy, it will also protect you and your family from food poisoning.

Safe cooking practices will depend on the type of meat you plan on cooking; some poultry or meat products need to be cooked all the way through; this means that the juice needs to run clear and there is no red or pink meat when you cut inside it. Some types of meats and poultry that you need to cook through includes:

- Rolled joints of meat
- Kebabs
- Sausages and rissoles
- Offal (including the liver)
- Pork
- All types of poultry and games like goose, duck, turkey, and chicken

However, there are also types of meats that you can eat that are cooked and rare or pink in the middle. Some of them include:

- Roasting cuts
- Cutlets

- Steaks

Clean cooking will depend on the quality and size of the meat cut. Therefore, you need to concentrate more on monitoring the temperature rather than the cooking time.

CHAPTER 3: PREPARING TO GO PEGAN

I t is not uncommon for people to start a Pegan diet today; it is the latest dieting rage. Can you eat meat? Yes, you can, but without exaggerating. What about processed ingredients? You can eat only a few. This diet mainly includes whole foods, which means you will be consuming fresh vegetables and fruits.

The Pegan diet combines both vegan and paleo diets, based on the belief that whole foods will support optimal health by reducing inflammation and balance blood sugar.

Upon first glance, the idea of combining vegan and paleo diets may seem contradictory or weird. However, you can rest assured that it is not. Instead, you should look at it as a compromise that brings together the best of both diets.

At its core, meal planning is very simple. As mentioned above, Pegan diet recipes contain small amounts of high-quality animal-based proteins, plenty of healthy fat, fruits, and vegetables. Additionally, you will have to give up legumes (peanuts, lentils, peas, and beans), grains, and dairy.

The tenets of the program shared by vegan and paleo diets include:

- Higher in quality fats: fats from olive oil, seeds, nuts, avocados, and omega-3 fatty acids
- Low in pesticides: Think organic, no hormones, antibiotics, and non-GMO foods
- No chemicals: No MSG, dyes, artificial sweeteners, or additives
- High quantity of vegetables and fruits: Look for deep and vibrant colors; the more the variety, the better

- Low glycemic load: Low on refined carbohydrates, flour, and sugar

When you decide to opt for the Pegan diet, you will:

- Consume sugary products sparingly; you can take them occasionally as a treat
- Avoid legumes, grains, and dairy
- Consume lots of seeds and nuts since they are rich in proteins and lowers the risk of diabetes and heart diseases
- Eat mostly vegetables, which should constitute about 75% of the daily diet
- Consume the right fats like omega-3, seeds, olive oil, nuts, and avocados; you should avoid soybean and vegetable oils
- Eat food with a low glycemic load; instead, look for more fats and proteins in foods like sardines, olive oil, seeds, nuts, and avocados.

Controversy

Since 2014, the popularity of Pegan recipes and diet has risen dramatically. For instance, searches for 'eating Pegan' rose to 337% in 2021 on Pinterest. However, this diet also has had its fair share of controversy.

For instance, experts suggested that the general parameters of this diet are simply taking two opposing diet ideologies and combining them into a new type of diet. However, in reality, they believe that most of the restrictions of a Pegan diet are time-consuming, costly, and unnecessary.

For example, limiting legumes may potentially be a problem, according to these nutritional and dietary experts. Based on studies, it has been found that legumes are low-fat, high-fiber, and a rich source of protein that is an important part of the much-popular Mediterranean diet. Additionally, legumes have been linked to several health benefits like the reduction of cardiovascular diseases, cancer, etc.

Positive Reports

While there have been some controversies regarding the Pegan diet, there are also several positive feedback. Experts agree that local and fresh is great; most of these experts agree with Dr. Hyman that animal-based products need to be consumed as a condiment, not the main course. Additionally, scientists also love the idea of increasing the intake of vegetables, fruits, and seafood.

Others have agreed that there are many aspects of a Pegan diet; for instance, the main pros of this diet are the emphasis on omega-3 fatty acids, fruits, and vegetables; additionally, there is also the factor of adequate protein.

The bottom line here is that a Pegan diet may prove to be great for your body. However, there are some types of restrictions that you will have to maintain. If you are able to do so, the Pegan diet will start having a positive effect on your body.

The Pegan Shopping List

Now that you know what you are up for, here are some products that definitely need to be on your shopping list:

- **Vegetables**: Your diet needs to contain vegetables that have a low glycemic index or starch; some examples would include tomatoes, peas, carrots, broccoli, mushrooms, leeks, eggplant, peppers, cauliflower, Brussel sprouts, greens (turnip, mustard, collard, etc.), bamboo shoots, etc.
- **Fruits**: Similar to vegetables, look for fruits that have low starch or glycemic index; these include pineapple, mangoes, pears, citrus fruits, dark berries, cherries, apples, oranges, watermelons, etc. Buy fruits that have high water content.
- **Animal Protein**: As long as the meat is grass-fed and sustainably sourced, you can consume various animal proteins like whole eggs, chicken, beef, pork, venison, etc. You can also consume seafood products like shrimp and salmon.
- **Healthy Fats**: For a Pegan diet, you have to stick to minimally processed fats from specific sources like nuts (except peanuts), seeds (except processed seed oils), coconut oil (unrefined), olives, and avocados (ensure the avocado and olive oil are cold-pressed), and omega-3 fatty acids (ensure the fish has low mercury content).
- **Oils and butters**: Since you cannot consume dairy products, you cannot consume conventional butter. There are a lot of options for butter like vegan butter, mashed avocado, etc. On the other hand, some types of oils include sesame oil, olive oil, etc. Avoid vegetable oils.

- **Dairy Replacement**: For a Pegan diet, some great dairy alternatives include hemp, almond, soy, cashew, hazelnut, and oat.
- **Sweeteners**: You can include some natural sugars in your diet like vanilla, dates, honey, coconut sugar, and maple syrup.
- **Nuts and Seeds**: Most nuts like almonds and walnuts, except for peanuts, can be consumed. As for seeds, you can depend on chia, pumpkin, and flax seeds for a healthy kick.
- **Legumes**: While legumes are normally discouraged in the Pegan diet, you are still allowed some gluten-free whole legumes in limited quantities. The intake should not be more than 75-grams per day. Some examples include pinto beans, black beans, chickpeas, and lentils.
- **Miscellaneous**: You can add various types of miscellaneous ingredients as long as they are low in the glycemic index level and natural.
- **Starches**: It is recommended that you limit the intake of starchy products. Even if you are consuming starch, ensure the sources are healthy.
- **Baking items**: For baking products, ensure the ingredients are without refined sugar and gluten-free. You can also add black rice, quinoa, oats, black beans, and chickpeas.
- **Supplements**: In the case of a Pegan diet, you can take supplements like Vitamin D3 and omega-3 fatty acids. You can also take Vitamin B12.

One-Week Pegan Meal Plan

A Pegan diet emphasizes vegetables and fruits; however, it also contains other types of ingredients like seeds, nuts, fish, and sustainably raised meats. You can also sparingly use gluten-free grains and some legumes. Here is a sample menu that you can cook for a week:

Monday

- **Breakfast**: You can cook a vegetable omelet with a simple green salad, topped with olive oil.
- **Lunch**: You can opt for a simple salad with avocado, strawberries, and chickpeas.
- **Dinner**: Wild salmon patties with lemon vinaigrette, steamed broccoli, and roasted carrots are perfect options for a dinner.

Tuesday

- **Breakfast**: Go easy with a sweet potato toast, topped with lemon vinaigrette, pumpkin seeds, and sliced avocado.
- **Lunch**: Cook a Bento box with blackberries, fermented pickles, raw vegetable sticks, sliced turkey, and boiled eggs.
- **Dinner**: Complete the day with vegetable stir-fry with black beans, tomato, bell pepper, onions, and cashews.

Wednesday

- **Breakfast**: Keep it healthy and simple with a green smoothie with hemp seeds, almond butter, kale, and apple.
- **Lunch**: Leftover vegetable stir-fry from Tuesday for an easy lunch.

- **Dinner**: You can have a rich dinner of vegetable kebabs, grilled shrimp, and black rice pilaf.

Thursday

- **Breakfast**: The best breakfast for this day would be chia seed and coconut pudding with fresh blueberries and walnuts.
- **Lunch**: A simple lunch for this day can be mixed green salad with cider vinaigrette, grilled chicken, cucumber, and avocado is the best choice.
- **Dinner**: You can opt for a delicious roasted beet salad with sliced almonds, Brussel sprouts, and pumpkin seeds.

Friday

- **Breakfast**: Braised greens, kimchi, and fried eggs are a good start for breakfast.
- **Lunch**: Keep it simple with vegetable stew and lentil with a side of sliced cantaloupe.
- **Dinner**: End the Friday with a salad with grass-fed beef strips, guacamole, jicama, and radishes.

Saturday

- **Breakfast**: Start your Saturdays with overnight oats, berries, walnuts, chia seeds, and cashew milk.
- **Lunch**: Have yesterday's vegetable stew and lentil for lunch.
- **Dinner**: Have a grand Saturday night dinner that consists of roasted pork loin with quinoa, greens, and steamed vegetables.

Sunday

- **Breakfast**: Have a lazy Sunday with a simple vegetable omelet and green salad.
- **Lunch**: Treat yourself to the Thai-styled salad rolls with orange slices and cashew cream sauce.
- **Dinner**: End the week with the previous night's pork loin and vegetables.

CHAPTER 4: PEGAN COOKING

H ere are some great recipes that you can cook as part of a Pegan diet:

Breakfast

1. Zucchini And Baked Eggs with Avocado

If you are looking for something more savory than sweet, then this dish is the perfect choice for you. Additionally, this dish is something that will not weigh you down a lot. This dish is high in protein and fat content and is considered a perfect breakfast. It is a delicious vegetarian breakfast recipe that is filling and flavorful. This dish is nutritious, easy to make, gluten-free, and Pegan-friendly that your entire family can enjoy.

Ingredients

- Non-stick spray
- Zucchini, 3, spiralized into noodles
- Extra-virgin olive oil, 2 tablespoons
- Black pepper and Kosher salt
- Large eggs, 4
- Red pepper flakes and fresh basil, for garnishing
- Avocados, 2, halved and thinly sliced

Cooking Instructions

1. You need to start by preheating the oven to 350°F. Next, lightly grease a baking sheet with non-stick spray.
2. Take a large bowl and toss in olive oil and the zucchini noodles into it; keep tossing until both ingredients mix properly. Season the mixture with pepper and salt.
3. Divide the noodles into four even parts and transfer the content into a baking sheet; ensure you shape the noodles like a nest.
4. Crack an egg and place it into the center of the nest; bake the dish until the eggs are set or until the timer hits 11 minutes.

5. Season the dish with pepper and salt. You can also use basil and red pepper flakes for garnishing. You can also serve the avocado slices along with it.

2. Olive Oil Baked Spinach, Egg, and Chickpeas with Sumac

This is a very simple and satisfying dish. Chickpeas are used in this dish, which is a sustainable and delicious source of protein. Chickpeas and olive oil are a winning pair. Additionally, the eggs make this dish heartier. It is hard to beat eggs when it comes to making breakfast. Apart from being filled with proteins, eggs can also help fight belly fat. This dish can be made with just a handful of ingredients that can be interchanged with whatever you like.

You can easily double this recipe by adding double the ingredients and cooking them on a larger iron pan. Even if you happen to make extra, you can eat the leftovers the next day. If you are having difficulty finding sumac, you can easily look for them online or at a specialty store. Or else, you can use other spices that you like – in this instance, cumin or coriander are great alternatives.

While the dish may look elegant, it is ridiculously easy to prepare. All you need to do is add everything in a single dish and put them in the oven. This dish also allows you to get creative by changing the spices or vegetables.

Ingredients

- Canned chickpeas, 14-15oz, rinsed
- Spinach, coarsely chopped
- Sumac, 1 teaspoon, optional
- Paprika, ½ teaspoon
- Sea salt, ½ teaspoon
- Black pepper
- Extra virgin olive oil, ½ cup
- Eggs, 2

Cooking Instructions

1. Preheat the oven to 425°F; on a small baking dish, add the spinach and the chickpeas.
2. On the same baking dish, add olive oil, pepper, salt, paprika, and sumac and place the bowl into the oven for five minutes.
3. Once done, crack the eggs over the chickpeas and place them back into the oven; bake for another 5-8 minutes. If the eggs are not cooked, bake for another two minutes.
4. Ensure the whites are cooked and the yolk is a little runny. If yes, you can top the dish with any topping of your choosing like pesto sauce, sliced avocado, sliced scallions, additional sumac, etc.

3. Vegetable Vegan Frittata

The vegan frittata is considered the best dish to make if you want to use the leftover vegetables to create an inexpensive and quick vegan meal. This delicious meal can be eaten for breakfast, lunch, or dinner.

A frittata is a dish that originates from Italy. It can be made with whatever vegetable you want and eggs. For this vegan frittata, a flavorful tofu-based 'egg' mixture and several other vegetables will be used.

Rarely will you find anyone that does not like frittata; it does not even matter at what time of the day you decide to cook this dish and eat it. Of course, this vegan frittata may not look the same as the egg version; however, it is still filled with a good amount of protein and fiber and has low cholesterol, which makes it a great vegan dish.

This tofu frittata is filling and flavorful. While it does not need much, you can also finish the dish with a drizzle of sriracha or avocado for some extra heat. If you have products that are about to expire in your refrigerator, you can use them to create this vegan dish.

Ingredients

- Potatoes, with or without skin
- Onions
- Bell peppers
- Zucchini
- Yellow squash
- Garlic
- Organic silken tofu, unpressed
- Unsweetened non-dairy milk
- Cornstarch, organic
- Nutritional yeast
- Mustard, whole grain, or dijon
- Tarragon, basil, or thyme
- Turmeric
- Garlic powder
- Pepper and salt
- Red pepper flakes

Cooking Instructions

1. Start by preheating the oven to 375°F.
2. Add the nutritional yeast, tofu, cornstarch, mustard, herbs, garlic powder, and red pepper flakes into a blender. Blend the mixture until the content has a smooth consistency. Scrape down the sides if needed.
3. Cut and cook the vegetables; once done, add the sauce from the blender and add it to the cooked vegetables.
4. Add the frittata mixture to a spring foam pan and place it in the oven. Bake the mixture for a good 45 minutes.
5. You can serve the frittata with sliced avocado for additional creaminess.

4. Baked Eggs in Tomato Cups

If you are looking for something extremely simple to cook, then you can consider this recipe. In fact, the simplicity of this recipe makes it one of the best ways to taste eggs from chickens that are organically fed cage-free and conventionally raised. While this recipe may not be very fancy, you can add this recipe to your breakfast menu. Alternatively, this dish can also be used as one of the sides for your lunch and/or dinner menu. This is a healthy, flavorful, and simple breakfast recipe.

Ingredients

- Tomatoes, 6
- Extra virgin olive oil, 1-2 teaspoons
- Ground pepper and salt
- Oregano, 1 teaspoon, dried
- Eggs, 6
- Fat mild cheddar cheese, 1/3 cup
- Fresh parsley, 1 tablespoon

Cooking Instructions

1. You need to start by preheating the oven to 350°F.
2. With the help of a cooking spray, grease a muffin tin and keep it aside.
3. Cut and remove the top of the tomatoes. With the help of a melon baller, remove the insides of the tomatoes. Keep them aside for different use.
4. Place the tomato cuts on a paper towel or plate and cut them side down. Let these stand for another ten minutes.
5. Place the tomatoes in the prepared muffin tin, cut side up. Add some olive oil to the tomatoes.
6. Season the tomatoes with pepper and salt. You can also add some dried oregano to the tomatoes.
7. Bake the tomatoes for 12 minutes. After that, remove them from the oven and crack an egg inside each of them.
8. Bake the egg-filled tomatoes for another 15 minutes, or until the eggs start to set. If you do not want runny or soft egg yolk, bake them for more than five minutes.
9. Add the cheese over the eggs and bake them until the cheese has melted.
10. Remove the contents and let it rest for two minutes. After resting, you can garnish them with parsley and serve.

5. Apple, Tofu, and Smoky Butternut Squash Breakfast Hash

Hash is a culinary diet that consists of chopped or diced meat, spices, and potatoes. All these ingredients are mixed and cooked with other ingredients like onions. For this recipe, butternut squash is used instead of sweet potatoes. The combination of apples and onions is considered a crowd favorite.

Instead of cooking it traditionally on a skillet, this recipe cooks it slightly hands-off; as a result, you get crispier squash. Once the dish is cooked, you will get a beautifully simple, autumnal breakfast dish. This dish is rich in proteins and can be customized with additional or different vegetables. For instance, you can take the liberty to experiment with rutabaga, collard greens, and parsnips.

Ingredients

- Natural vegetable oil like refined avocado or grapeseed, 2 tablespoons
- Butternut squash, 1-1/4 ounces, seeded, peeled, and cut into cubes
- Small apples, 1-2 pieces
- Tofu, 8 ounces
- Smoked paprika, ¾ tablespoon
- Low-sodium tamari or coconut amino, 1 tablespoon
- Onion, 1, chopped
- Brussel sprouts, 3 cups, shaved
- Apple cider vinegar, 1-1/2 tablespoons
- Pepper and salt
- Whole grain toast, hot sauce, optional

Cooking Instructions

1. First, preheat the oven to 400°F and line the baking sheet with foil or parchment. Add one tablespoon of oil, apple, and squash in a pan and toss it.
2. Transfer the mixture to the baking sheet and add pepper and salt. Keep roasting the apple and squash for at least 35 minutes, or until they become crisping at the edges and tender.
3. Add the remaining oil into a deep and large skillet over a medium flame. Add the tamari/coconut aminos, smoked paprika, and tofu cubes and cook them. Ensure that you stir frequently. Drop in the Brussel sprouts and cook them until they are tender and crisp.
4. Once ready, fold the roasted apples and squash and add the vinegar. Mix and stir all the ingredients properly and add pepper and salt according to taste. Do the same for the vinegar.
5. Once the dish is done, you can serve it with hot sauce or whole-grain toast.

6. Sheet Pan Breakfast Fajitas

Sheet pan breakfast fajitas are considered one of the best breakfast recipes for a Pegan diet. These fajitas are packed with onion, various bell peppers, perfectly baked eggs, and seasoning. Perhaps the best part of this recipe is that everything is done directly on the sheet pan so that you do not have to use anything else. Cooking this recipe is very basic; all you need to do is chop up the vegetables, season them, and bake them in the oven until they are soft.

Apart from being simple to cook, this dish is also packed with vitamins and nutrients like lutein, Vitamin B12, and Vitamin E.

Ingredients

- Red bell pepper, 1, thinly sliced
- Green bell pepper, 1, thinly sliced
- Orange bell pepper, 1, thinly sliced
- Olive oil, 2 tablespoons
- Chili powder, 1 tablespoon
- Garlic, 3, minced
- Lime juice, 1 tablespoon
- Paprika, 1 teaspoon
- Cumin, 1-1/2 teaspoons
- Onion powder, ¼ teaspoons
- Pepper and salt
- Eggs, 6
- Avocado, 1, peeled, seeded, halved, and sliced
- Cilantro leaves, ¼ cup, chopped

Cooking Instructions

1. Begin preheating the oven to 400°F. Meanwhile, coat the baking sheet with nonstick spray or lightly oil it.
2. Place all the bell pepper variants on the baking sheet and stir in onion powder, paprika, cumin, garlic, lime juice, chili powder, and olive oil. Keep tossing until the mixture combines properly; add salt and pepper for taste.
3. Place this mixture into the oven and bake for approximately 12-15 minutes, or until the contents become tender.
4. Remove this mixture from the oven and create six wells into it. Start adding the eggs; ensure that you do it very delicately and keep the yolk intact. Season the dish with pepper and salt according to taste.
5. Keep the mixture back into the oven and bake it for another 10 minutes, or until the egg whites have settled down.

6. Serve the dish immediately; you can garnish it with cilantro or avocado, based on your preferences.

7. Roasted Vegetable Bowl

This roasted vegetable bowl is a great recipe that you can serve for a hearty breakfast. Alternatively, you can also eat this dish for lunch and/or dinner. This is a delicious, easy, and healthy recipe that you can cook and serve quickly. Since this dish contains a lot of vegetables, it is safe to say that it is filled with a lot of minerals and nutrients needed by the body.

Ingredients

- Yellow or red baby potatoes, 3-4, sliced into ¼-inch rounds
- Sweet potato, ½, sliced into ¼-inch rounds
- Beet, 1 medium, sliced into 1/8-inch rounds
- Carrots, 2, halved and sliced
- Melted coconut or avocado oil, 2 tablespoon
- Curry powder, 1 teaspoon
- Radishes, 4, halved or quartered
- Cabbage, 1, thinly sliced
- Sea salt, ½ teaspoon
- Red pepper, 1
- Broccoli, 1 cup
- Kale or collard greens, 2 cups

For topping:

- Lemon, 1, juiced
- Tahini, 2 tablespoons
- Hemp seeds, 2 tablespoons
- Avocado, ½, optional

Cooking Instructions

1. Similar to the above, start by preheating the oven to 400°F. Use parchment paper to line two baking sheets.
2. On one of the baking sheets, add the radishes, beets, carrots, sweet potatoes, and potatoes and drizzle them with sea salt, curry powder, and oil. Keep tossing the mixture until they combine properly and bake them in the oven until they become tender and golden brown, or for 25 minutes.
3. Add the broccoli, bell pepper, and cabbage to the second baking sheet and drizzle it with the remaining salt, curry powder, and oil. Toss and combine these ingredients nicely.

4. After the potatoes and carrots mixture gets roasted, bake the second mixture for roughly 20 minutes. When the timer is at the last five minutes, add the kale or collard greens until they are either bright green or roasted.
5. Divide the vegetables into appropriate servings with the toppings like hemp seeds, tahini, and lemon juice. Garnish the dish with avocado (optional); alternatively, you can also use any other fresh herbs for the garnishing.

Soups and Salads

As for soups and salads, some great Pegan recipes include:

1. Bone Broth, Chicken, and Vegetable Soup

This is a delicious and immune-boosting soup that you should eat once every 2-3 days. This is the perfect dish if you are battling flu, have a cold, or simply need some warming up during the colder months. This soup has a lot of things going on – it has chicken bones, garlic, turmeric, and shiitake mushrooms – it is safe to say that these ingredients are full of nutrients.

In terms of nutrition, shiitake mushrooms are absolute powerhouses. At times, they are also known as beta-glucans, which supports and encourages the growth of good bacteria in the guts. If your gut has good bacteria, your immune system will improve and you will have a better life.

Ingredients

- Whole chicken, 1, (2-3 lbs) or chicken bones, 2-3lbs
- Bulb garlic, 6 cloves
- Yellow onion, 1, sliced
- Carrots, 3, chopped
- Shiitake mushroom, 1-1/2 cups or 12, sliced
- Celery stalks, 2, chopped
- Turmeric, 1-inch, peeled and chopped
- Fresh ginger, 1-inch, peeled and chopped
- Parsley, 1 pack
- Peppercorns, ½ teaspoon
- Sea salt
- Water, 10 cups
- Baby spinach, optional

Cooking Instructions

1. You can start by placing all the ingredients, except for the water, into a large pot

2. Next, pour water into the pot until all the ingredients are just submerged, not overflowing. This should be roughly ten cups of water.

3. Start boiling the ingredients; cover the pot with a lid and let it simmer.

4. Skim the top of the soup after half an hour to remove the non-edibles that can be seen on the top.

5. Let the pot simmer for a minimum and maximum of two and six hours, respectively

6. Once done, sieve the soup to filter the chicken and vegetables from the soup; additionally, the extra chicken meat can be used for other types of dishes. Sieve the soup twice.

7. Add chicken meat, mushrooms, and carrots (optional) to the broth while serving.

2. Sheet Pan Potato and Golden Beet Soup

This soup is perhaps the easiest soup that one can make. All you need to do is roast the vegetables of your choice and pour them into a pot. You can also add some blend or broth. You do not have to stand over the stove stirring the pot and filling your kitchen with steam.

Perhaps the best part of this dish is that you do not even have to be an accomplished chef. All you need to do is roast these vegetables. However, you do need to be careful so that you do not over roast the ingredients.

Ingredients
- Golden beets, 2 lbs, peeled and chopped
- Avocado oil, 2 tablespoons
- Russet or Yukon gold potatoes, 2 large, peeled and cut
- Yellow onion, 2, peeled and chopped
- Water, 4 cups
- Garlic cloves, 4, peeled
- Pepper and salt
- Lemon juice, 1 tablespoon

For toppings:
- Hemp hearts
- Sprouts
- Fresh dill
- Sliced radishes
- Avocado

Cooking Instructions

1. The oven needs to be preheated to 400°F. Cut the beets into
    ½-inch pieces so that they can bake quickly. Place them on a
    baking tray, drizzle some oil, and toss them to mix them
    properly. Roast them for ten minutes; it is okay if they
    darken or turn black.
2. While the beets are getting roasted, chop the potatoes into
    1-inch pieces. Chop the onions as well.
3. Add them both and whole garlic cloves into a separate
    baking tray. Drizzle some oil and toss to coat. After the
    beets are done, add the second tray into the oven. Now,
    roast both trays for another 30 minutes.
4. After the vegetables and beets become tender, add them
    into a blender. Also add pepper, salt, and water into the
    same. Blend the mixture properly.
5. Once done, you can add the lemon juice and top them with
    any topping of choice.

3. Thai Mango Avocado Salad with Sweet Potatoes

This is one of the best soup dishes that you can have. It consists of grilled potatoes and has a tangy flavor. This is a perfect summer dish that is free of gluten. The mango will give the soup a juicy and sweet burst while the avocado will add creaminess and smoothness to the mix. Additionally, the fish sauce/lime juice, smoky-sweet potato, and cucumber will all seal in a flavor profile that you will definitely feel on your tongue.

Ingredients

- Sweet potatoes, 1 medium, peeled and sliced
- Coconut oil, 1 tablespoon
- Mango, 1 cup
- Avocado, 1, cubed
- Cucumber, 2/3 cup, diced
- Fresh mint, ¼ cup, thinly sliced
- Cilantro, ¼ cup, diced

For the sauce:

- Fresh lime, 4 teaspoons
- Fish sauce, 2 teaspoons

Cooking Instructions

1. First, you need to preheat the grill to very hot heat.
2. Next, toss the sweet potato pieces into the grill; toss them in coconut oil first and grill them until you see grill marks on them or roughly four minutes.
3. After the pieces have cooled, cut them into small cubes and add them into a bowl.
4. Add the cilantro, mint, cucumber, avocado, and mango, and keep stirring the mixture until it combines properly.

5. Mix in the fish sauce and lime juice in a small bowl and pour them over the salad. Keep tossing them for proper mixing and add salt for seasoning.

4. Black Rice and Roasted Tomato Salad with Pesto

This salad is unconventional; it means that instead of adding raw vegetables, you roast them instead. This dish is perfect for anyone who is trying to switch to a Pegan diet. This salad is full of nutrition and gluten-free. Even if you cannot finish it, you can use it as a side dish.

Ingredients
• Black rice, ¼ cup
• Water, ¾ cup
• Pesto without cheese, ¼ cup
• Cherry tomatoes, 300-gm
• Roasted red pepper, ½
• Pumpkin seeds, 1 tablespoon
• Lettuce, 2 cups
• Orange, ½
• Pomegranate seeds/arils, ¼ cup
• Goat cheese, 50-gm
• Arugula/rocket leaves, 10
• Olive oil, 1 tablespoon
• Lemon juice, 1 tablespoon
• Salt

Cooking Instructions

1. You need to cook the black rice per instructions. Even if you cannot soak it overnight, you should rinse it at least 2-3 times. Place the rice in the cooker and cook the rice for about 15 minutes.
2. After the rice is cooked, transfer the rice to a colander and rinse it with cold water. Ensure it is completely dried before you use it further in the salad.

3. Preheat the oven to 392°F. Grease two baking sheets with olive oil.
4. Place the pumpkin seeds in a bowl and add salt and olive oil. Cover the seeds completely and place them on one of the baking sheets.
5. Mix the tomatoes with salt and olive oil and place them on the second baking sheet. Make sure that there is some space between each tomato piece.
6. Rub the red pepper with olive oil and place them in a tray with the tomatoes. After eight minutes, remove the seeds and transfer them to a bowl so that they do not continue to roast.
7. Remove the tomatoes from the heat and place them in a separate bowl. Meanwhile, roast the peppers for another 35 minutes. After the roasting is done, remove and peel them.
8. To make the salad bowl, place the shredded lettuce and stir in the red pepper, roasted tomato, and cooked place rice. Add salt according to preference.
9. Add the arugula leaves to the salad. Add the goat cheese, pomegranate arils, and seeds. Drizzle some olive oil as well.

5. Southwest Chicken Soup

Also known as the detoxifying southwest chicken soup, this particular dish is a simple vegetable and chicken soup with many detoxifying ingredients. If you want to get your digestive system back on track, you can eat this soup for several days in a row.

This soup is gluten-free, paleo, low carb, and low fat; it works like a charm if you want to cleanse your digestive system. The combination of green chilies and spices enhances the flavor of the vegetables and chicken if you are looking for a tantalizing bold flavor. When it comes to taste, this soup can definitely pack a punch. Additionally, you do not have to be a Masterchef to learn how to prepare this simple and delicious soup.

Ingredients

- Chicken breasts, 1-1/2 lbs, skinless and boneless
- Large onion, 1, peeled and chopped
- Garlic, 4 cloves, minced
- Olive oil, 1 tablespoon
- Green chilies
- Tomatoes, 14.5-ounces, fire-roasted and crushed
- Chicken stock, 3 quarters
- Cumin, 1 tablespoon
- Turmeric, ½ teaspoons
- Crushed red pepper, 1 teaspoon
- Carrots, 2-1/2 cups, sliced
- Cabbage, 4 cups, chopped
- Broccoli florets, 3 cups
- Avocados, 2, peeled and diced
- Pepper and salt

Cooking Instructions

1. Place a large pot over medium heat and add olive oil, garlic, and chopped onions. Sauté the mixture until the ingredients become soft, or for five minutes.
2. Add the chicken breasts, carrots, spices, broth, crushed tomatoes, green chilies, and salt into the mix.
3. Lower the heat and let the mixture simmer for 20 minutes. Ensure that the chicken breasts are cooked through. Using a

pair of tongs, remove the chicken and place them on a cutting board.

4. Add broccoli and chopped cabbage to the pot and continue to simmer until the broccoli becomes soft. Meanwhile, shred the breasts and add the pieces back into the soup.

5. After the broccoli becomes tender, add salt according to your taste. Add the avocado while serving.

6. Quinoa Pegan Salad Bowl

This quinoa salad bowl is a pegan-friendly option. Since this dish does not contain any grains, it has a reduced carb load. Being a seed, quinoa provides the required protein content. Additionally, the vegetables do not contain starch and low-calorie content. This salad is a flavorful light salad that is perfect for your lunchbox and pleasing for the eyes as well.

One main tip here to cook the black beans is to soak them overnight and pressure cook them for four minutes. Additionally, ensure that you allow the steam to escape normally and drain the liquid naturally. You can use this liquid as stock or for kneading dough.

Ingredients

For the salad:

- Quinoa, 1 cup, cooked
- Black bean, ½ cup, cooked and drained
- Cabbage, ½ cup, shredded
- Onion, ¼ cup, chopped
- Cucumber, ½ cup
- Baby spinach leaves, 1 cup

For the dressing:

- Black pepper
- Lemon juice, 3 tablespoons
- Miso paste, 1 tablespoon

Cooking Instructions

1. To begin with, you need to wash and cook the quinoa. Once done, set it aside to cool down.
2. Collect all the other ingredients for the salad; wash them properly and drain them.
3. Start chopping the cucumber and onions; shred the cabbage as well. Once done, add them into a bowl and arrange them on different sides.
4. Wash and drain the black beans and add them to the bowl.
5. Take the quinoa and add it to the bowl.
6. Whisk the lemon juice, miso, salt, and pepper for the dressing. Add this dressing over the salad and toss if desired.

7. Buddha Bowl

This peculiar bowl is a great option if you are looking for Pegan-based salads. This vegetable consists of vegetables, quinoa, and eggs, which makes it a perfect recipe if you are looking for something that is light and healthy. This salad does not contain processed ingredients and additives. These vegetables do not contain any starch.

Ingredients

- Button mushroom, 300 grams, sautéed
- Asparagus, 200 grams, sautéed
- Boiled eggs, 6
- Quinoa, 1-1/2 cups, sautéed
- Red capsicum, 1
- Zucchini, ½
- Iceberg lettuce, 1 head
- Colored cabbage, ¼ cup, optional
- Onions, 2, chopped
- Garlic, 8 cloves, minced
- Red chili powder, ½ teaspoon
- Salt
- Cherry tomatoes, 15-20
- Carrot sticks, 1 cup
- Pumpkin seeds

Cooking Instructions

1. First, you have to add the mushrooms and water together to wash away the grit. Add the eggs to the water to boil and also add salt. In another pan, add quinoa and water and start bowling it as well.
2. Start cutting the vegetables. Chop the onions and mince the garlic. Cut and dry the mushrooms in an even size. Peel the asparagus and chop the broccoli.
3. Once the eggs are boiled, peel and set them aside.
4. Add the salt and quinoa to the boiling water and mix it well. Ensure the flame is on the low setting.
5. Add the onions, garlic, and salt to the mushroom. Also, add some chili powder and set it aside.

6. Drain the eggs and add water and broccoli to the same pan; keep steaming the broccoli until it becomes edible.
7. Take a saucepan and add olive oil and garlic. Keep roasting this mixture until the raw smell disappears. Add the asparagus now and keep sautéing it until it is done.
8. Add the rest of the onions, garlic, and oil and sauté. Add the cooled quinoa to the mix.
9. Add lettuce leaves, sautéed quinoa, eggs, vegetables, and mushrooms to serve.

Snacks and Starters

Some great snacks and starters would include:

1. Sautéed Collard Green Omelet

You can now enjoy your collard greens by converting them into a delicious snack. This dish has been rated as one of the best and can easily make your tongue shout out. It does not matter how you have prepared the collard. The point of this dish is to have well-seasoned and savory cooked greens. With the help of these greens, bacon or American pancetta, and some chipotle sauce, this omelet is definitely something to remember.

Ingredients

- Butter, 3 tablespoons
- American pancetta or Double smoked bacon, ½-inch or 4 oz, respectively
- Hearty greens like beet greens, dandelion greens, mustard greens, collard greens, 1 lb, stems removed
- Water, chicken stock or vegetable stock, ¼ cup
- Chipotle hot sauce
- Pepper and salt
- Chardonnay vinegar
- Eggs, 4
- Parsley, finely chopped

Cooking Instructions

1. On a nonstick pan, add the butter and let it melt. Next, add the pancetta and cook it until it is crispy and golden brown; it should not take more than ten minutes. Additionally, the fats need to be rendered.
2. Add the vinegar, hot sauce, and the greens and cook for about five minutes, or until the greens start to wilt.
3. Season with pepper and salt and add some stock if the greens start drying before getting soft.

4. Add butter to another nonstick pan and heat it over medium flame. The butter needs to start shimmering.
5. Whisk the eggs in a bowl until it has a fluffy and light consistency. Add some pepper and salt according to taste. Pour the eggs into the butter.
6. Let the eggs cook; once done, push the eggs into the center of the pan with a rubber spatula to let the liquid egg cook. Keep repeating until there is no liquid left.
7. Place the greens under the center of the egg and roll it in a cylindrical shape. Season it with pepper and salt and garnish the dish with parsley.

2. Pan-Seared Salmon with Apple Salad and Kale

While this dish may look very fancy, it is very easy to prepare and cook. You can easily have it as a mid-day or evening snack. The salmon does not take more than ten minutes to cook in the skillet. Additionally, the flavors of the crunchy kale simply meld into the fish. All you need to do is add the whole-wheat roll and the dish is ready to serve. This dish is sweet, tangy, and crunchy.

Ingredients

- Salmon fillets, 4
- Fresh lemon juice, 3 tablespoons
- Olive oil, 3 tablespoons
- Salt and pepper
- Kale, 1 bunch, leaves thinly sliced and ribs removed
- Dates, ¼ cup
- Honeycrisp apple, 1
- Pecorino, ¼ cup, finely grated
- Slivered almonds, 3 tablespoons, toasted
- Whole wheat dinner rolls, 4

Cooking Instructions

1. Before cooking, get the salmon fillets to room temperature.
2. In a pan, whisk together the salt, olive oil, and lemon juice. Add the kale and toss it to mix it properly. Let it stand for ten minutes.
3. Meanwhile, cut the apples into matchsticks and dates into slivers. Add the almonds, cheese, apples, and dates to the kale. Season the mixture with pepper, toss it and set it aside.
4. Sprinkle some peppers and salt into the salmon. Take a nonstick skillet and add the remaining oil over medium flame. Place them skin-side up salmon into the pan and raise the heat. Cook for about four minutes or when the salmon becomes golden brown on one side.
5. Flip the salmon and keep cooking it for another three minutes or until it becomes firm.
6. Place the salmon, rolls, and salad on a plate to serve.

3. Grilled Vegetables with Creamy Cilantro Dip

If you like grilled vegetables, then this is the perfect recipe for you. This dish can also be consumed by people that want to lose weight. This dish is gluten-free and does not contain any dairy. The vegetables are only marinated in a dressing that is made with green chilies, ginger, garlic, and olive oil. As for the goat cheese, it is optional.

Ingredients

- Button mushrooms, 7-8 pieces
- Red onion, 1 cup, cubed
- Bell peppers, 1 cup, cubed
- Cherry tomatoes, 7-8
- Zucchini, ½ cup, thickly sliced
- Green chilies, 1-2
- Ginger, 1 piece
- Garlic cloves, 5-6
- Mint leaves, 1 teaspoon
- Olive oil, 1-2 tablespoon
- Raw agave or any other plant-based sweetener, ½ teaspoon
- Red chili powder, 1 teaspoon
- Cumin powder, ½ teaspoon
- Dry mango powder, ½ teaspoon
- Goat cheese
- Turmeric powder, ¼ teaspoon
- Salt, as per taste

For the avocado cilantro dip:

- Avocado, 1
- Fresh cilantro, 1 cup
- Lemon juice, 1 tablespoon
- Garlic cloves, 1-2
- Green chilies, 1-2
- Salt

Cooking Instructions

1. Take the mushrooms and wash and pat them. If they are big, cut them into smaller pieces.
2. Take the ginger, garlic, and green chilies and add them to a mortar. Keep grinding them until they become smooth. Instead of green chilies, you can also use fresh mint leaves.
3. Take oil, spice powders, sweetener, paste, goat cheese, and lemon juice. Add and mix them well.
4. Cut the vegetables into cubes and marinate them into this mixture. Use your hands for this.
5. Cover the bowl with a lid or cling film. Keep it in the refrigerator for one hour.
6. Once an hour, grill the vegetables on all sides. If using the oven, preheat the oven to 200°F and grill the vegetables for 10 minutes. Set the vegetables aside once done.
7. Now, you can start making the avocado and cilantro dip. Start by adding the ingredients to the chopper or blender and keep blending it until it has a smooth consistency.
8. Serve the vegetables with this dip.

4. Mexican Roasted Cauliflower

Most people would consider the Mexican roasted cauliflower as one of the best starters, especially if you want to follow a Pegan diet. These cauliflower florets are tossed in delicious spices and roasted until they are caramelized and crispy. This dish can be served with red onions, cilantro, and lime juice. This dish is vegan and gluten-free.

However, there are some precautions that you definitely need to take. For instance, the cauliflower florets will get mushy and soft if the oven is not hot enough; this means that the final dish will not be caramelized and crisp. Also, you need to ensure that the baking pan is not over-crowded; if this happens, the florets will steam even before it starts to crisp up.

Ingredients
• Cauliflower head, 1 large, cut into florets
• Avocado oil, 2 tablespoons
• Chili powder, 1 teaspoon
• Onion powder, ½ teaspoon
• Garlic powder, ½ teaspoon
• Cumin, ¼ teaspoon
• Salt, ¾ teaspoon
• Cilantro, ¼ cup
• Black pepper, ¼ teaspoon
• Red and green onion, ¼ cup, diced
• Avocado, ½, sliced
• Lime wedges, 3

Cooking Instructions

1. Start by preheating the oven to 425°F. Next, add the cauliflower florets with pepper, salt, cumin, onion powder, garlic powder, chili powder, and avocado oil. Mix the ingredients properly.
2. Line the baking tray with parchment paper and spread the cauliflowers evenly. Roast for roughly 20 minutes.
3. Remove from the oven and flip the cauliflower. Roast the next sides until the edges become crispy or for another 10-12 minutes.
4. Remove the cauliflower from the oven and garnish them. You can serve the cauliflowers with avocado, lime wedges, onion, and/or fresh cilantro.

5. Caveman Chicken And Vegetable Roast

This caveman chicken and vegetable roast is considered a delicious sheet pan meal that can be eaten by your family and friends. Regardless you are dieting or not, this dish is extremely delicious and easy to cook.

The roasted vegetables are a perfect complement to the chicken drumsticks. When combined together, they make for an easy and tasty weeknight meal. The vegetables in this roast consist of parsnips, onion, potato, and carrots. These veggies are roasted along with the garlic cloves and the chicken. The seasoning mix consists of standard kitchen staples like ground black pepper, salt, and dried thyme leaves.

Roasting the concentrates of the vegetables extracts their sweetness and makes them very tender as well.

You also have the choice to season the dish with other types of spices and herbs. This is a great dish because it can be thrown together and does not require a lot of work. All you need to do is add the ingredients together and let your oven do the rest of the work.

Ingredients

- Onions, 1, peeled and cut
- Garlic, 12 cloves
- Russet potato, 1
- Parsnip, 1
- Baby carrots, 1 cup
- Chicken drumsticks, 1-1/2 pounds, skin on
- Olive oil, ¼ cup
- Apple cider vinegar, 1 tablespoon
- Dried thyme leaves, 1 teaspoon
- Salt, 1-1/2 teaspoons
- Ground black pepper, ½ teaspoons

Cooking Instructions

1. Start by preheating the oven to 400°F. Combine all the ingredients on a large rimmed baking sheet. Toss and mix properly.
2. Place the mixture in the oven and roast it until the vegetables are tender and the chicken is cooked through, or for roughly an hour.
3. In the midway, remember to stir. Serve the dish immediately.

6. Prosciutto Wrapped Asparagus

There is no doubt that asparagus and prosciutto are a heaven-made match. The earthy and nutty flavor of the asparagus spears can only be complemented by the crispiness and saltiness of the ham. They can be broiled in an oven under a grill, pan-fried, or grilled on a barbeque. This dish is a great choice for entertaining guests. It can also be served as a starter dish for any type of party. You can also dip these sticks in soft-boiled eggs, instead of the regular toasted bread.

While this dish is extremely simple to make, you need to be careful as well. Always ensure that the prosciutto is of good quality and paper-thin. It is suggested that you pre-wrap the asparagus with the prosciutto before the arrival of your guests.

Ingredients

- Olive oil
- Prosciutto strips/slices, 6
- Asparagus spears, 12

Cooking Instructions

1. You need to wash the asparagus and cut them at 2-cm off the ends. As for the prosciutto, cut them into two halves; this way, you will end up with 12 strips.
2. Place each of the prosciutto strips at 45-degrees on a chopping board. Place the asparagus on the top of the prosciutto and it should be perpendicular to it.
3. The tip of the asparagus should be on the same line as the bottom of the meat strip. Wrap the bottom of the prosciutto over the asparagus spear so that the meat is held tight.
4. From here, you can start rolling the asparagus in the upward direction. Since it is at a 45-degree angle, the prosciutto strip will start covering the entire spear from the bottom up. Even if it does not cover the entire asparagus, it is nothing to be worried about.
5. Add some oil to a frying pan and wait until it is sizzling hot. Fry these prosciutto-wrapped asparagus for a minute or two, or until the prosciutto becomes crispy and brown.

7. Thai Chicken Lettuce Cups

The Thai chicken lettuce cup is considered one of the best healthy dishes today. Also known as LarbGai, this dish can be made very easily and full of fresh flavors, thanks to lime and various herbs. This dish is quite popular in Asian countries because they are absolutely fabulous.

This dish is a celebration of textures and flavors. It has the perfect balance of spiciness, sour, savory, and sweet, with the fresh crunch of the lettuce and the heat from the aromatic herbs. Similar to other types of Thai cuisines, these lettuce cups are all about fresh flavors. There are not a lot of ingredients in the sauce – just a bit of fish sauce and lime juice. Much of the flavor comes from the mix of other aromatics like lemongrass, chili, garlic, and ginger, which are sautéed until the dish becomes golden. At this stage, it starts to smell very delicious, even before adding the chicken, fresh herbs, and sauce.

Ingredients

- Minced chicken, 450g
- Red chilies, 2, de-seeded and chopped finely
- Garlic, 2 cloves, minced
- Lemongrass stalk, 1, finely chopped
- Ginger, 1-inch, grated
- Fish sauce, 2 tablespoon
- Lime juice
- Fresh coriander and mint
- Lettuce leaves, shaped like gems

Cooking Instructions

1. Add the olive oil to a frying pan or wok. Add the ginger, lemongrass, garlic, and chili and cook them for a minute.
2. Add the minced chicken into the mixture and cook until through or for another four minutes.
3. Add some lime juice and fish sauce to the mix. Cook until the flavors start combining.
4. Add the mix to the washed lettuce cups and sprinkle the dish with thin strips of red chili, coriander, and/or chopped mint.

Entrees

If you are looking for some great Pegan entrees, you can consider the list below:

1. Turmeric Sautéed Greens

Most people have no idea that turmeric is good for their health. Even more do not know how to add it to their dish. Thankfully, this particular dish is one of those that is easy to make and incorporates turmeric as well.

When we make smoothies, we add some turmeric to them. One of the best aspects of it is that it has a very strong flavor; however, it is not overpowering, which is why even children love it. Apart from smoothies, turmeric can also be used in a wide range of dishes, like this turmeric sautéed greens.

It is no secret that turmeric has been consumed for centuries now. It has all types of healthy and natural benefits as well as natural anti-inflammatory properties. Simply by adding turmeric to various dishes, you will receive a lot of healing powers that you may require.

Ingredients
- Olive oil, 1 tablespoon
- Garlic, 3 cloves, minced
- Fresh turmeric, ½-inch
- Swiss chard, spinach, or kale, 2 bunch each, thinly sliced
- Kosher salt, ¼ teaspoon
- Water, 2 tablespoons

Cooking Instructions

1. Before slicing the greens, ensure that you have to wash them properly. Once the washing and cleaning are done, mince them thinly.
2. In a large saucepan, add some oil and start heating it in medium flame.
3. Add salt and the greens of your choice and start sautéing for a minute.
4. Pour the water into the pan and keep cooking it until the greens of your choice are just wilted
5. Transfer the contents into a bowl and serve.

2. Japanese Sticky Chicken

The Japanese sticky chicken is one of the most flavorsome dishes to prepare and cook. It is perfect if you are looking for a recipe that is quick, easy, and family-friendly.

Chicken is considered one of the most versatile sources of proteins today and is also very kid-friendly. However, it is all about what you can do with it. This peculiar dish has a salty and sweet taste that will make you drool and have your fingers 'licking good'.

This dish is very versatile and you can easily replace some of the ingredients to create something unique. Even if you cannot eat the entire dish in one go, the leftovers will be just as delicious as the ones you have had the previous night. Some prefer serving this chicken dish with brown rice and salad, thereby making it a perfect summer meal.

Ingredients

- Fresh ginger, 1 tablespoon
- Mirin, ¼ cup
- Honey, ¼ cup
- Low sodium soy sauce, ¼ cup
- Rice vinegar, 1 tablespoon
- Sesame oil, 1 tablespoon
- Togarashi spice blend, 1 teaspoon
- Skin-on chicken breasts, 2 bone-in
- Skin-on chicken legs, 4 bone-in
- Scallions, 3, chopped

Cooking Instructions

1. In a baking dish or large zipper bag, add and whisk the Togarashi spice blend, sesame oil, rice vinegar, soy sauce, honey, mirin, and ginger.
2. Add the chicken pieces to this mixture and keep turning the pieces. Marinade the chicken for an hour in the refrigerator or leave them overnight.
3. Preheat the chicken to 450°F and place the marinated chicken in it.
4. Keep the chicken skin side up and bake it until it is golden brown or for 30 minutes.
5. For serving, sprinkle the dish with scallions.

3. Smoked Salmon Scramble

Salmon is considered one of the best sources of omega-3 fatty acids, which instantly makes it a healthy choice for your family. This recipe is very easy to prepare and can be a perfect protein-rich breakfast or dinner. Additionally, you can also serve it with fresh fruit, bagels, or orange juice as a weekend brunch for your entire family.

Smoked salmon can be purchased in any two forms – cold smoked and hot smoked. Cold smoked salmon is not cooked and has a very creamy and delicate texture. On the other hand, hot smoked salmon is cooked during the smoking process, thereby giving it a salty taste.

Cooking scrambled eggs should be very easy, as long as you follow the rules. Ensure that the eggs are uncracked and clean for safety reasons. When you break them into the bowl, please look into it that no shells are broken into the eggs. It is suggested that you beat the eggs only just before cooking them. Also, use canola oil only, which will add a distinctive flavor to the dish.

For this dish, we have used hot smoked salmon. However, you can also use cold-smoked salmon; but, it will remain tender and soft. For the best texture and flavor, it is recommended that the dish be served immediately.

Ingredients

- Eggs, 8
- Chives, 4, chopped
- Kosher salt, ½ teaspoon
- Canola oil, 2 teaspoons
- Salmon, 4, smoked and thinly sliced

Cooking Instructions

1. Reserve two slices of salmon for the garnishing; as for the remaining two, chop them up in very small pieces
2. Whisk the eggs with some chives and season them with salt.
3. Preheat a pan and add the eggs to it. Keep scrambling the eggs and ensure that they do not dry out.
4. Once the eggs have been cooked together but not dried, add the chopped salmon. Place the pan on a trivet after removing it from the stove.
5. Garnish the eggs with the remaining chives and salmon and it is ready to serve immediately.

4. Asian Cauliflower Rice

This Asian cauliflower rice is considered a great choice for entrees, thanks to a lot of reasons. For instance, this dish is bright in color. Additionally, it consists of a lot of vegetables as well. Of course, you have the choice of adding various types of vegetables to this dish; the choice is up to you.

Ingredients
• Avocado oil, 1 teaspoon
• Eggs, 3
• Sesame oil, 1 tablespoon, toasted
• Avocado oil, 3 tablespoons
• Red onion, 1, small and diced
• Ginger, 2 teaspoons
• Cauliflower, 3 cups, riced
• Broccoli, 8-ounces, cut into florets
• 2 carrots diced
• Crimini mushrooms, 6-ounces, chopped
• Asparagus spears, 6, chopped into 1-inch pieces
• Snow peas, ½ cup, chopped
• Garlic cloves, 8, minced
• Red bell pepper, 1, diced
• Black pepper, 1 teaspoon
• Kosher salt, 1 teaspoon
• Onion powder, 1 teaspoon
• Sesame seeds
• Green onions
For the sauce:
• Coconut aminos, 1/3 cup
• Toasted sesame oil, 1 tablespoon
• Rice vinegar, 1 tablespoon
• Fish sauce, 1 teaspoon

Cooking Instructions

1. Add the avocado oil into a sauté pan and wait for it to become hot. In the meantime, whisk the eggs and add them into the pan once the oil becomes hot. Cook until the eggs are just soft, remove them, and set them aside. Clean the pan to remove residual eggs.
2. Add the sesame oil and the remaining avocado oil to the pan and start heating. Add diced onion and sauté until they are soft, or for five minutes. Add the minced garlic and stir for another minute.
3. Add the asparagus, mushrooms, carrots, broccoli, and riced cauliflower and cook them until they become soft. Drop the rest of the ingredients, pepper, salt, and garlic into the mixture and cook well.
4. While the vegetables and rice is being cooked, you can prepare the sauce. Whisk all the sauce ingredients together. After the rice and vegetables are cooked, stir in the sauce and lower the heat.
5. Once the sauce becomes saturated, add the cooked eggs into the mix. Serve immediately with green onions and sesame seeds.

5. Lemon Roasted Chicken and Caramelized Vegetables

This lemon roasted chicken with caramelized vegetables is a true dinner entrée for many reasons. All you have to do is roast the ingredients; voila! Your delicious meal is ready. It is definitely one of the best dishes that you can cook with chicken.

Even if there are leftovers, the chicken pieces will be more delicious than before because the flavors get mixed even more and the chicken still remains juicy and moist underneath the skin. Of course, you cannot deny the tangy flavor of roasted lemons.

Ingredients

- 5-pound chicken, 1
- Lemon juice, 1 lemon, do not discard
- Garlic cloves, 6, peeled and left whole
- Fresh thyme, 20 sprigs, divided
- Fresh parsley, 5 sprigs
- Fresh rosemary, 2 sprigs
- Olive oil, 3 tablespoons
- Dried tarragon, ½ teaspoon
- Dried thyme, ½ teaspoon
- Salt, ½ teaspoon
- Pepper, ½ teaspoon
- Baby potatoes, 1-1/2 lbs
- Carrots, 1-1/2-lbs, peeled and chopped into 1-inch pieces
- Large onion, 1, coarsely chopped
- Additional salt and pepper for the vegetables

Cooking Instructions

1. The first step is to preheat the oven to 400°F. In the meantime, wash and rinse the chicken, remove the giblets from the cavity, pat dry, and remove the extra fat.
2. Add salt and pepper to the chicken.
3. On the outside of the chicken, pour the lemon juice. Also, add the garlic cloves and lemon halves.
4. Tie the rosemary, parsley, and fresh thyme sprigs together and place them inside the chicken, along with the garlic and lemon.
5. Rub the olive oil on the chicken. Mix the salt, pepper, thyme, and dried tarragon in a small bowl and rub the mix over the chicken layer. Tie the legs and wings together.

6. Once the chicken has been prepped, place it on a large sheet pan, only after an hour at room temperature.
7. Combine the onions, carrots, potatoes, and the remaining oil in a large bowl and season it with salt and pepper. Spread the vegetables around the chicken and place the remaining thyme sprigs around the vegetables.
8. Roast the chicken in the oven for an hour. Before slicing, let it sit for 15 minutes. Serve hot.

6. Southern Style Pork Tenderloin

Most people consider that cooking pork takes a lot of time, especially certain parts like the tenderloins; in fact, this particular dish can be cooked well within 20 minutes, if you do not consider the marinating part. One of the best things about this dish is that you can cook the remaining marinade and serve it as a sauce. Additionally, you also have the choice to serve the pork with some sweet corn on the cob, mixed vegetables, or garlic mashed potatoes.

Ingredients

- Soy sauce, ¼ cup
- Bourbon, ¼ cup
- Dijon mustard, ¼ cup
- Brown sugar, ¼ cup
- Olive oil, 3 tablespoon
- Fresh ginger, 1 tablespoon, finely chopped
- Garlic cloves, 3, minced
- Pork tenderloins, 2 whole, trimmed

Cooking Instructions

1. Place the soy sauce, bourbon, brown sugar, olive oil, and Dijon mustard in a bowl and start whisking it. Pour the mix into a glass container or a large zipper bag.
2. Add the pork tenderloins into the container or zipper bag and let it marinate for a night or two.
3. On the day you want to cook the pork, preheat the oven to high heat and keep the grates oiled.
4. Remove the pork from the container or bag and start grilling them for 14-15 minutes. Once the internal temperature reaches 140°F, turn it halfway. Reserve the rest of the marinade.
5. Remove the pork from the grill and let it sit for some minutes. While the meat is being rested, boil and reduce to simmer the marinade and cook for ten minutes.
6. Slice the tenderloin as per wishes and serve the pieces with the marinade sauce.

7. Spiced Chicken with Olives and Lemon

As mentioned previously, chicken is considered one of the most important sources of proteins today. Thankfully, you can create a lot of different dishes with chicken. This spiced chicken with lemon and olives is one of the delicious choices.

This dish is a native of the mountainous region of Morocco; however, you do not have to travel to this region to try this tasty dish out. It is very simple and can be cooked in no more than 20 minutes. You can also use other varieties of vegetables and spices based on your taste and preferences.

Ingredients
• Garlic, 5 cloves, finely chopped
• Saffron threads, ¼ teaspoon, pulverized
• Ground ginger, ½ teaspoon
• Sweet paprika, 1 teaspoon
• Ground cumin, ½ teaspoon
• Turmeric, ½ teaspoon
• Salt and ground black pepper
• Chicken, 1, cut in 8-10 pieces
• Extra virgin olive oil, 2 tablespoons
• Onions, 3, thinly sliced
• Cinnamon stick, 1
• Calamata olives, 8, pitted and halved
• Cracked green olives, 8 pitted and halved
• Large or small preserved lemons, 1 or 3 respectively
• Chicken stock, 1 cup
• Lemon juice, ½ lemon
• Flat-leaf parsley, 1 tablespoon, chopped

Cooking Instructions

1. Mix the turmeric, cumin, paprika, ginger, saffron, and garlic in a bowl. If you are not using kosher chicken, add some salt as well. Combine and apply the mixture on the chicken layer, cover it, place it in your refrigerator, and let the chicken marinate for 2-3 hours.
2. Add some oil to a skillet and heat it. Add some onions and cook it for 15 minutes. If you are using one, transfer the mix to a tagine or simply leave it in the skillet. Add the cinnamon stick.
3. Remove the chicken from the refrigerator and place it on the skillet with the onions. Scatter the olives as well.
4. Remove the pulp of the lemon and cut the skin in strips; once done, add them to the chicken. Also, mix in the lemon juice and the stock.
5. Cover the skillet or the tagine. Place it over low heat and cook until the chicken is done, or for 30 minutes. As for serving, scatter the parsley on the top.

Sides

The recipes of some amazing Pegan sides include:

1. Raw Almond Dip

This simple and delicious raw almond dip is a great choice if you are looking for a Pegan hummus. When these almonds are blended, they create a creamy and delicious spread. It is naturally gluten-free, vegan, low-carbohydrate, and raw, thereby making it a great option when it comes to catering to a lot of people at a party.

There are several reasons why this almond dip is a much better option if you are opting for a healthy lifestyle. Almonds are very high in minerals and vitamins and protect the cells from oxidative stress. They also contain a good amount of Vitamin B2, copper, manganese, and magnesium.

Ideally, it is important that you soak the almonds before using them. Apart from helping blend better, it also removes phytic acid compounds that are present and bind with minerals like calcium, zinc, and iron and make them less bioavailable for the body. You should soak them for at least six hours; the ideal time is 12 hours.

Ingredients

- Raw almonds raw, 1 cup soaked
- Extra virgin olive oil, ¼ cup
- Raw tahini, ¼ cup
- Water, 3/4 cup
- Garlic, 2 cloves
- Lemon juice, ¼ cup
- Salt, ½ teaspoon
- Pepper ground, ½ teaspoon
- Cumin, ¼ teaspoon
- Turmeric powder, 3/4 teaspoon
- Parsley, ¼ cup, optional

Cooking Instructions

1. You first need to soak the almonds in water for at least six hours; the preferable time is 12 hours. Before using the almonds, ensure that you dry them first.
2. Add all the above-mentioned ingredients into a blender and keeping blending it until the mixture has a smooth consistency. Keep tasting and adjusting the seasoning. If you are looking for flavor and color, you can add parsley.
3. You can serve the hummus with various types of dishes.

2. Vegan Zucchini Rotis/Tortillas

These vegan rotis/tortillas are perfect if you are looking for sides that are dairy-free and low-carb. This dish is very easy to make and free of allergens. They can also be made in advance and stored for next-day meals; you can simply reheat them and enjoy them whenever you want.

As most of us already know, zucchini is a very healthy vegetable. It does not have a lot of carbs. Additionally, some other ingredients of this dish include almond flour, nutritional yeast, psyllium husk, and chia seeds, which are all vegan products. While it is recommended that you make use of blanched almond flour for making the rotis/tortillas, you can also make use of coconut flour.

Ingredients

- Zucchinis, 3, grated
- Chia seeds, 1 tablespoon, coarsely powdered
- Psyllium husk, 2 tablespoon
- Nutritional yeast, ¼ cup
- Blanched almond flour, 2 tablespoon
- Salt and pepper

Cooking Instructions

1. Wash and dry the zucchini and pat them dry. Grate the zucchini using a food processor or box grater.
2. Take the chia seeds and add them to a spice or coffee grinder. Once you grind them, add psyllium husks.
3. Add the chia seeds powder, grated zucchini, psyllium husk, and salt and pepper in a large bowl. Add the nutritional yeast as well. Mix and combine well to prepare the dough.
4. To prepare the dough, add some almond flour as well. Allow the mixture to stand for ten minutes.

5. Now, you can start baking the rotis/tortillas. Start by preheating the oven to 350°F.
6. Take a baking sheet and grease it. Take a small portion of the dough and start making a ball of it.
7. Press the ball on the baking sheet to flatten it so that you can create thin discs for roti or tortilla.
8. Bake each roti/tortilla for ten minutes on both sides each. After 20 minutes, the tortillas will be cooked nicely, with slightly brown edges.

3. Sweet Potatoes with Lemony Kale and White Beans

This sweet potato with lemony kale and white beans is the perfect side dish that can go with any type of meal. Creating this side dish from scratch is very easy and can be done within minutes. Additionally, it can also be used as a salad topping. Of course, kale and sweet potatoes are considered some of the most expensive vegetables in the market. However, this dish is totally worth the cost.

When you consume dishes that do not have a lot of calorie content, you do not increase your calorie count. If you are an active person, you can also add some tofu or chicken to this dish and increase the number of pumpkin seeds. Try out this dish and you will be very satisfied with the taste.

Ingredients

- Sweet potatoes, 4, medium/large
- Olive oil, 1 tablespoon, optional
- Shallot or onion, 1, chopped
- Garlic, 1 to 2 cloves, minced
- Lemon zest cost, 1 teaspoon
- Sea salt, 1-½ teaspoon
- Kale, 1 bunch, thick stems removed and chopped (alternatively, you can also use spinach, chard, baby kale, collards, etc.)
- Cannellini beans, 1 can
- Crushed red pepper flakes, 1-1½ teaspoon, optional
- Lemon juice
- Toasted tamari pumpkin seeds

Cooking Instructions

1. Start by preheating the oven to 350°F. Meanwhile, wash and dry the potatoes and prick the top a few times with the help of a fork.
2. Take a sauté pan and start preheating it; add the oil and cook the shallots for two minutes. Add the lemon zest, garlic, and salt and stir it for another minute.
3. Add the red pepper flakes, beans, and kale and cook for another three minutes. Add the lemon juice and taste for seasoning.
4. Remove the pan and allow the sweet potatoes to cool. Place them on top of the bean and kale mixture and also add the pumpkin seeds.

4. Spiralized Sweet Potato Crust Vegetable Pizza

This is a tasty and mouth-watering pizza that is made up of vegetables. The crust consists of spiralized potatoes that have been baked to perfection. Additionally, you can also add a wide range of vegetables on the top, based on your taste and preferences.

This is a type of pizza that will redefine the meaning of a vegetarian pizza. It is a nutritious and filling dish that is grain-free, paleo, vegan, and gluten-free. It is a perfect twist for any traditional pizza night.

Ingredients

- Sweet potato, 1, large and spiralized
- Large Brussels sprouts, 3, quartered
- Large bell pepper rings, 3
- Flax eggs, 2
- Baby radishes, 3, sliced
- Nutritional Yeast, 1-2 tablespoons

For the sauce:

- Unsalted tomato paste, 2 tablespoon
- Minced garlic, ½ teaspoon
- Dried oregano, 1 teaspoon
- Onion powder, ½ teaspoon
- Dried basil, ½ teaspoon
- Dried marjoram, ½ teaspoon
- Black Pepper, ¼ teaspoon

Cooking Instructions

1. Begin the cooking process by preheating the oven to 450°F. Mix the spiralized sweet potato to the flax egg and make use of your hands.
2. Mix the ingredients for the sauce in a small bowl.
3. Grease a baking dish, baking sheet lined with Silpat or parchment, or cast-iron skillet and place the potato right at the center. Ensure that the potatoes are in a circular shape.
4. Add the sauce with the help of a spoon on the crust of the pizza. Add the vegetables to the next layer and sprinkle some nutritional yeast.
5. Place the pizza in the oven and cook for 15 minutes. Make use of a spatula and remove it from the plate to serve.

Desserts

Some delicious Pegan dessert recipes include:

1. Pegan Apple Crisp

The fall season is considered the best time to eat fruits like apples, pumpkins, and pomegranates. With the help of apples, you can create a delicious Pegan apple crisp, which is a nutritious twist on the traditional apple crisp dish. This recipe is filled with nutritious and whole ingredients that do not include artificial sugar. It is a perfect dessert recipe that will allow you to eat a sweet treat while also loading up on some nutritious ingredients like gluten-free oats, grass-fed ghee, and apples.

There are a lot of reasons most people love apples. These fruits are known to provide a lot of nutritional benefits. One of the most unique aspects of apple is that it is packed with both soluble and insoluble fiber, which is important to maintain a healthy gut. The fiber present in apples feeds the short-chain fatty acids present in the gut, which helps in energy production in the large intestines.

Ingredients

- Apples, 2, halved and cored
- Almond flour, 1/4 cup
- Gluten-free oats, 1/2 cup
- Grass-fed ghee, 2 tablespoons
- Brown sugar, 1/4 cup

Cooking Instructions

1. Preheat your oven to 350°F.
2. On a baking dish, place the apples, with the carved/cored portion facing upward.
3. Mix the brown sugar, almond flour, and oats in a small bowl. Combine well.
4. Add this combination to each of the halved apples until they are full.
5. Top each apple/oat mixture with the ghee.
6. Place the apple/oat mixture in the oven and bake until they are fully cooked and soft, or for 40 minutes approximately.

2. Vegan Paleo Brownies

This vegan paleo brownies recipe is considered one of the fastest and easiest desserts that you can make. This is a sweet dessert that will not make you feel guilty, whatsoever. Additionally, it will not cause you to gain weight. These brownies will be very crisp, have a deep chocolate flavor, and will be fudgy as well, depending on how long you keep them in the freezer.

Ingredients

- Melted coconut oil, ½ cup
- Cocoa powder, ½ cup
- Unsweetened dark chocolate, 2-4-oz.
- Maple syrup, ¾ cup
- Flax eggs, 2 (or actual eggs, if you are not vegan)
- Vanilla, 1 teaspoon
- Coconut flour, ¼ cup
- Salt, ½ teaspoon

Cooking Instructions

1. Start by lining a 12-pocket muffin tin with parchment paper liner and preheat the oven to 350°F.
2. Combine the unsweetened chocolate, cocoa powder, and coconut oil in a saucepan and heat it over medium flame. Keep whisking it until the mix becomes consistent and smooth.
3. Remove the mix from the heat and add the maple syrup (or you can also use honey). You will see that the mixture will slowly start thickening.
4. Add the vanilla and flax eggs and combine well.
5. Add in the salt and coconut flour. Ensure that you keep combining until there are no dry pockets.
6. Pour the mix into the prepared pan and bake it for 20 minutes.
7. Once the baking is done, let it cool down and then transfer it to a freezer. However, if you are looking for something like a lava cake, then there is no need to transfer it to the freezer. For brownies, the freezer is important as it will give it consistency and texture.

3. Strawberry Coconut Smoothie

Perhaps the best aspect of this strawberry coconut smoothie is that it can be consumed as both breakfast and dessert. This is a breakfast/dessert smoothie that will be filled with nutrition and keep you energetic. When you have the smoothie after a heavy dinner, it will help with the digestion process as well. The prep instructions are very simple and the smoothie will be ready within a few minutes.

Ingredients

- Coconut milk, 1 cup
- Banana, 1 cup, frozen and sliced
- Strawberries, 2 cups, frozen
- Vanilla extract, 1 teaspoon
- Vegan-friendly protein powder, 1 scoop, optional

Cooking Instructions

1. Add all the ingredients to the mixture and start blending until it has a very smooth consistency.
2. Keep adding coconut milk until the mix becomes thick according to how you like it.
3. Serve with ice.

4. Pegan Pancakes with Coconut Whipped Cream

These pancakes can be eaten as a breakfast item or after-dinner dessert. These pancakes consist of healthy ingredients and are also very easy to make. There are no weird ingredients, apart from nutritious ones.

Ingredients

For the pancakes:

- 2 large eggs
- Unsweetened almond milk, 1-½ cups
- Pure vanilla extract, 2 teaspoons
- Coconut oil, ¼ cup, melted
- Granulated monk fruit sweetener, 3 tablespoons, optional
- Raw pecans, ¼ cup, crushed
- Buckwheat flour, 1 cup
- Almond flour, ½ cup
- Baking powder, 1 teaspoon
- Baking soda, ½ teaspoon
- Sea salt, ¼ teaspoon
- Ground cardamom, ¼ teaspoon
- Ground cinnamon, 2 teaspoons
- Ground cloves, ½ teaspoon
- Ground nutmeg, ½ teaspoon
- Ground ginger, ¼ teaspoon
- Pure maple syrup, optional

For the whipped cream:

- Coconut cream, 14-ounces, chilled overnight
- Monk fruit, 1/3 cup, powdered

Cooking Instructions

1. Beat the almond milk, egg, coconut oil, vanilla extract, and monk fruit sweetener in a bowl until the eggs are fully mixed and fluffy. Add the crushed pecans.
2. Sift the almond flour, buckwheat, salt, baking soda, cardamom, cinnamon, nutmeg, and cloves in another bowl. Once done, transfer the mix to the wet mixture and keep stirring until all the lumps disappear.

3. Take a large skillet and start heating it. When it is hot enough, brush the pan with the remaining coconut oil and pour some of the batters into it. Let the mixture cook for two minutes on both sides. Ensure that the pancakes are crispy and golden brown on both sides. Repeat the process for the rest of the batter.

4. To make the whipped cream, you first need to cool a large mixing bowl. Remove the coconut cream from the freezer and scoop out the solid cream portion. Mix it until it is creamy and add the powdered monk fruit and the remaining cinnamon. Mix again for two minutes.

5. Serve the pancakes with the whipped cream. If you want, you can also add sliced figs and a drizzle of maple syrup on the top.

Conclusion

Now, it is time to conclude this book – let us review what we have learned from the above. A Pegan diet is considered one of the most popular types of diets today. It combines the eating style of two other popular diet types – the paleo and the vegan diets. Since these two types of diets have unique strengths, you get the best of both worlds with a Pegan diet. While most of the foods on your plate will consist of vegetables and fruits, animal-based products will only be eaten as side dishes. Additionally, this diet also focuses on whole foods that are nutrient-dense to support optimal health, balance blood sugar, and reduce inflammation. A Pegan diet is not designed as a short-term diet. If you want to see the difference, it needs to be long-term and sustainable.

CPSIA information can be obtained
at www.ICGtesting.com
Printed in the USA
LVHW080407211021
701042LV00002B/103